They called him insane.
They said he would never write another novel
because he had burned out his brains with drugs.

THEY WERE WRONG.

Philip K. Dick went on to write
A Scanner Darkly and four VALIS novels,
which are considered some of his best work.

While producing some of his best fiction,
he also labored on a monumental work
of nonfiction that he called Exegesis.

All that we have are his notes and correspondence,
based on visions, dreams and insights,
because he did not live long enough
to compose the finished work.

Let's explore what he did accomplish
in formulating his Exegesis.

MORE ON THE X IN EXEGESIS:
Philip K. Dick's Religious Speculations
A Work in Progress
by Tessa B. Dick, M.A.

The author holds a Master of Arts in English Literature and a Bachelor of Arts in Communications from Chapman University, as well as an Associate of Arts in Foreign Language from Fullerton College. Mrs. Dick, who was married to Philip K. Dick, taught English and Communications at Chapman University for 12 years before retiring. She has also taught at National University and Riverside Community College, in addition to serving as a substitute teacher in K-12 for the Riverside Unified School District.

AUTHOR'S NOTE: Quotes from *Exegesis* are from *The Exegesis of Philip K. Dick*, Pamela Jackson and Jonathan Lethem, Editors, New York: Houghton Mifflin Harcourt, 2011, unless otherwise specified. Bible verses are from the King James Version, unless otherwise specified.

PREFACE

Philip K. Dick's monumental work, which he called *Exegesis*, is more properly called *Eisegesis*. That is, rather than interpreting the text in its own context, he was reading his own context into the text. For the most part, he ignored the culture of the writers and readers of the original Scriptures and imposed his own worldview onto the text.

His unflagging work on the *Exegesis* began with his visionary experience of 1974, which more than a few of his friends and colleagues interpreted as confirmation of the rumors that he had gone insane. They wondered whether this was the result of years of drug abuse, or simply the outcome of the many experiences of existential pain which he had suffered throughout his life. In actuality, the visions began early in his life and reached the summit of enlightenment in 1974. He considered those visions a gift from the Holy Spirit, who would rescue him from the ersatz world where he had suffered so much. He also noted in 1976, "It is bootless to screw around and think it is anyone but Christ who arranged my 3-74 experience" (*Exegesis*, p. 212). This is not a contradiction, since the Holy Spirit and Christ are both members of the Trinity.

One of the main points that Phil made regarding Christianity was that the cross of the Crucifixion was shaped like the letter X, not the letter T. However, he was almost certainly mistaken about the shape of the cross. In a letter to Patricia Warrick in 1981, Phil wrote, "Now Tree X, which has been seen at two times and in two places, although still recognizable as Tree X is conceived as a recurring constant, and it is around Tree X that reality is organized . . ." (quoted in Don Herron, Editor, *The Selected Letters of Philip K. Dick, 1998-1982*. Nevada City, CA: Underwood Books, 2009, p. 114). In conversations, he associated the tree with the cross, referring to Acts 5:30,which says in several translations that Jesus was hanged on a tree. Here are two examples from translations of the Bible that Phil owned:

> The God of our fathers raised up Jesus, whom ye slew and hanged on a tree. (King James Version)

> The God of our ancestors raised Jesus to life after you killed him by hanging him on a tree. (International Standard Version)

Thus, to his mind, the tree was the X-shaped cross. He probably came closer to the truth when he compared the Christian fish symbol to the helical spiral shape of DNA. In any case, he pursued the unknown, which we abbreviate as the letter X, as we do when solving equations in algebra. And, of course, we could be watching *The X-Files* on television or streaming it on the internet, but Phil never watched that program because it first aired more than a decade after he passed away. However, he was aware of the Hammer science fiction horror film *X, the Unknown*, which premiered in 1956. He was also aware that people would call him insane

when he spoke in public about his experiences. For
example, his now famous speech in Metz, France, was
not well received in 1977, but today it inspires people
and ranks very high in the number of YouTube views it
receives.

Philip K. Dick did not go insane in 1974; he simply
gathered the courage to speak in public about things he
had experienced throughout his life. The Exegesis
chronicles his exploration of what those experiences
might mean for him, personally, and for the wider world.

~~~
~~~

CHAPTER ONE: GNOSTICISM AND THE END TIMES

Oddly for a man who claimed to be a faithful Episcopalian, Philip K. Dick focused much of his work on the pagan myths, especially those of Greece and Rome. He also delved into Gnosticism and Eastern mysticism, but he always came back to the God of the Bible. In his *Exegesis*, he wrote, "I didn't *earn* my salvation and verdict of innocence, however; Christ rendered me innocent by guiding me into innocence" (Pamela Jackson and Jonathan Lethem, Editors, *The Exegesis of Philip K. Dick*, New York: Houghton Mifflin Harcourt, 2011, p. 539). Gnostics, on the other hand, generally believe that you achieve salvation by gaining knowledge, not as a gift from Christ or God.

Phil gathered from reading the Encyclopedia Britannica that gnosticism was a dualist religion. For example, in the article on Plotinus (the founder of Neoplatonism who lived in the third century A.D.) he read, "So e members of Plotinus's circle of friends were gnostics (heretical Christian dualists who emphasized esoteric salvatory knowledge)" (A. Hilary Armstrong, "Plotinus", https://www.britannica.com/biography/Plotinus). Unfortunately, to call gnostics "dualist" is an oversimplification of their beliefs. According to Stephan A. Hoeller (Tau Stephanus, Gnostic Bishop), "In the Gnostic view, there is a true, ultimate and transcendent God, who is beyond all created universes and who never created anything in the sense in which the word 'create' is ordinarily understood. While this True God did not fashion or create anything, He (or, It) 'emanated' or brought forth from within Himself the substance of all there is in all the worlds, visible and invisible." Thus, Gnosticism cannot be dualistic, since it proclaims one God. (Stephan A. Hoeller (Tau Stephanus, Gnostic Bishop), "The Gnostic World View: A Brief Summary of Gnosticism," *The Gnosis Archive*, http://gnosis.org/gnintro.htm).

Many bits and pieces of Phil's experience and writing do reflect Gnostic theology. For example, he dreamed about a swarm of bees joyously flying when they remembered their divinity, "the recovery of awareness of identity" (*Exegesis*, p. 215). However, he interpreted this dream not as a Gnostic revelation, but in terms of Hinduism: "Bees buzzing and floating in unison equals restored parts of the Brahman" (ibid.).

He often claimed that his experience was Gnostic, in the sense of the Gnostic sects of the second and third centuries of this era, but that experience and his interpretation of it did not conform to Gnostic theology. In fact, his own words reveal that Phil did not understand Gnosticism, even while he professed a belief in and acceptance of it. For example, he repeatedly referred to the "Gnostic trinity", but there is no such thing. The closest to a concept of a triune Godhead in Gnosticism comes down to us from Valentinus, who lived about 100 to 160 A.D. A comment by Marcellus implies that he developed a primitive concept of the trinity "in a work that he entitled *On the Three Natures*" (Bentley Layton, "Valentinus, Fragment B", *The Gnostic Scriptures*. New York: Doubleday, The Anchor Bible Reference Library, 1987).

Unfortunately, the Valentinus text has not survived, so all we have is the comment by Marcellus of Ancyra. Moreover, Valentinus was most likely exploring the threefold nature of man, not the three aspects of God:

> Another Valentinian text that shows the division of humanity into three types is the *Tripartite Tractate*, which says that the arrival of the Savior meant that humanity "came to be in three essential types, the spiritual, the psychical, and the material." These correspond to those whose response is immediately positive, those who are hesitant, and those who "shun" saving knowledge. (Peter Kirby, "The Threefold Nature of a Lost Valentinian Text", October 6, 2013. http://peterkirby.com/the-threefold-nature.html)

In fact, the idea that man has three natures comes down from Plato, who was a major influence on Valentinus. While the Greek/Roman philosopher Plutarch (more or less a contemporary of Valentinus and also strongly influenced by Plato) wrote about the threefold nature of Sophia (John M. Dillon, *The Middle Platonists, 80 B.C. to A.D. 220*. New York: Cornell University Press, 1996, p. 388), the Gnostic Sophia is not God, not a member of the Trinity, but simply a lower Emanation from the One (God) in Gnostic theology. To Phil's mind, Sophia was the feminine aspect of God.

Different sects of Gnosticism disagreed on minor points, but all agreed on the existence of the One, that is, one

God. In fact, they were monist; that is, they believed that not only was God everywhere, but everything was a part of God. Therefore, Valentinus and other Gnostics almost certainly did not believe in a triune Godhead, so Phil was mistaken about that and other facts, probably due to his reliance on secondary sources. While the *Encyclopedia Britannica* and the many volumes of history written by Will and Ariel Durant provide adequate starting places for research, Phil rarely went beyond them. To be fair, we must take into account that we have access to far more primary sources now than we did in the 1970s. Most primary sources could be found only in university libraries, not at the local bookstore or the community library, and of course there was no internet. He did own several books about the Nag Hammadi texts, as well as the Dead Sea scrolls, but those writings were still in the early stages of translation and publication.

Phil thought of Sophia as a member of the Judeo-Christian Trinity. To his mind, she was God's Holy Wisdom, equivalent to the Holy Spirit or to the Tora. Sophia's name does mean wisdom in Greek, but in Gnosticism she is a foolish minor deity who unwittingly causes our suffering. She later feels sorry for Adam, who was created as a slave to evil deities, so she puts a spark of the divine into him. However, the One (God) does not, as Phil thought, come down to our world and kick out the evil god who made this world and caused our suffering. In fact, the One is a thing, not a person, and it does not care about us (Stephan A. Hoeller (Tau Stephanus, Gnostic Bishop), "The Gnostic World View: A

Brief Summary of Gnosticism," *The Gnosis Archive*, http://gnosis.org/gnintro.htm).

Most of us are left to suffer, while the souls of the few elite Gnostics (all men, no women) rise into the heavens to join the Gnostic pantheon of Emanations (Aeons) when they die. On the other hand, Phil did share the Gnostic (also Platonic) concept that this world is not real, that it is an illusion and we are trapped in the prison of material reality. Gaining knowledge about the true world, in his view, can set us free from what he called "the Black Iron Prison".

His interpretation of Scripture was more in line with dualistic religions like Zoroastrianism than with Gnosticism. We can see this in the first entry of his "Tractates Cryptica Scriptura" at the end of his novel *VALIS*: "One Mind there is; but under it two principles contend." He goes on to describe a battle between light and darkness, and to depict our world as an illusion formed from false information, which can be restored through the power of true information. The darkness clouds our minds, preventing us from seeing the world as it really is, while the light enables us to see clearly. As Paul said in 1 Corinthians 13:12, "For now we see through a glass, darkly, but then face to face: now I know in part; but then shall I know even as also I am known." This Bible verse (I Corinthians 13:12) inspired the title of Phil's 1977 novel *A Scanner Darkly*.

Today's Gnostics often claim Philip K. Dick as one of their own, but Gnosticism is not a dualistic religion. Phil sometimes claimed to agree with Gnostic ideas, but he did not fully understand Gnosticism. In fact, Gnostics believe in one God, a force that resides above the universe. This "good" God does not do battle against the "evil" god. This God is not a person, and it is not the Creator, and it does not engage in the battle between light and darkness or good and evil. It probably does not even know that we exist. In fact, Gnosticism describes a pantheon consisting of Emanations from the One God (Aeons), and one of these Emanations gives birth to the Creator, who is Yahweh. This world is filled with evil, pain and suffering because the Creator is evil. Various Gnostic sects disagree on the details of their theology, but all agree that there are many gods and one supreme God, the One. Dualism, on the other hand, describes a battle between two gods. Moreover, in Gnosticism, Jesus and Christ are two different Emanations, and Jesus is not the Son of God.

Phil often dated the beginning of a world-wide deception, a matrix or simulation, to the first century A.D., when Jesus was crucified and his followers were oppressed. "The empire never ended" has become a sort of code, letting others know that you agree with Philip K. Dick that the Roman Empire still rules the world today, at least as a template for contemporary tyrannical regimes. Similarly, the phrase "Black Iron Prison" connotes the state of involuntary servitude in which many people believe we live. His insistence that our world is delusional does fall in line with Gnosticism, but he maintained the belief that God will rescue us from the evil deity who misleads us. Gnostics rely upon secret knowledge for their salvation.

The X became a symbol of resistance against the Empire in Phil's mind. In fact, it holds more importance in his work than the fish sign employed by early Christians, the fish sign that inspired his 1974 visions. However, when the X appeared to him as a glowing red and gold letter, it was more than the letter X. He tried to draw it for me, and I recognized it in hindsight while researching early Christianity, particularly the conversion of the Roman Emperor Constantine and the Council of Nicea.

Phil's vision of the "X" was the Chi-Rho, which he said that he saw in a March 1974 vision:

More about the Chi-Rho will be discussed in a later chapter of this book.

Phil drew his idea about the End Times and the return of the Savior from reading about Albert Schweitzer, and possibly from reading some of Schweitzer's own writing. In a book in his personal library, Phil read a sketch of Schweitzer's view of Jesus. In part, it says that Jesus "expected his parousia within a few weeks. But it did not happen" (A. Powell Davies, *The Meaning of the Dead Sea Scolls*, New York: New American Library, 1956). The *parousia*, which means appearance and carries the connotation of the Second Coming, or at least of the revelation that Jesus is the Messiah, did not happen, so Jesus was mistaken, according to Schweitzer. He was not the Messiah, after all.

Philip K. Dick developed his own interpretation of Schweitzer's observation about the events recorded in the Gospels. Jesus and his disciples expected the End Times to come within their lifetime, and the end has not arrived, so time must have stopped. We are still living in the first century A.D., and the modern world that we see around us is an illusion. The powers of darkness, who wish to keep us in their thrall, have deluded us into believing that time and history have progressed over the past two thousand years. Of course, the traditional interpretation is that the prophecy delivered by Jesus at the Mount of Olives was fulfilled in 70 A.D., when Emperor Titus put down the Jewish rebellion and the Temple in Jerusalem was destroyed. (see Matthew 24 & 25; Mark 13; Luke 21)

Phil's personal religious beliefs center on dualism, which is more consistent with Zoroastrianism or Manichaeism than with Gnosticism precisely because he envisioned a cosmic battle between good and evil personified as powerful deities. Phil was also familiar with the Marcion heresy, which posits the existence of two gods; the loving God of the New Testament seeks to rescue us from the wrathful God of the Old Testament

who created us. Of course, the heresy promoted by
Marcion inspired antisemitism in its time (the second
century A.D.).

Zoroaster's exact date is disputed, but he probably lived
around 700 B.C. He wrote scriptures in which he
formulated a battle between two gods: the god of light
(Ahura Mazda) and the god of darkness (Ahriman).
Mani (the founder of Manichaeism who lived in the
third century A.D.) borrowed that dualistic concept and
combined it with ideas culled from Gnostic Christianity,
Buddhism and other sources. Like Plato and the
Neoplatonists (e.g. Plotinus), Mani believed that matter
is an evil manifestation of the darkness. Since our bodies
are material, we are trapped in evil bodies. For Plato,
material objects were mere shadows on the wall of the
Cave. For Philip K. Dick, material objects were chains
in the Black Iron Prison.

~~~
~~~

CHAPTER TWO: MADMAN, PROPHET OR BOTH?

In his Ph.D. thesis, Andrew Mark Butler states that Philip K. Dick's science fiction fulfills some of the criteria of realism (Chapter 1, p. 12). He goes on to describe realism in terms of three factors:

> There are therefore several versions of literary realism which may be described. The simplest level is where a realistic novel is a mimetic novel: it is a text which is an attempt to represent the real world. Alternatively, a realistic novel is one which uses certain patterns of conventional behaviour, which are familiar to the reader, and which therefore appear to be realistic. Finally there is the sense that a given work of fiction resembles another work of non-fiction; non-fiction is assumed to be an accurate reflection of reality. In all three cases there have to be elements of recognition, agreement or consensus: that the novel does represent the real world, that the behaviour described is conventional or that it does resemble it.
> (Butler, "Ontology and Ethics in the Writings of Philip K Dick." University of Hull, 1995, Chapter 1, pp. 13-14)

I propose that Phil was writing about his own real, personal experiences of the strange and unusual. In other words, his literary style was realism in the sense that it was real to him. He had paranormal and spiritual experiences which he attempted to describe in his works of fiction. Moreover, he encountered glitches in our shared reality throughout his life, beginning decades before his mystical experiences of 2-3-74. Thus, his proper literary genre is realism, rather than or in addition to science fiction.

On the other hand, Angus Taylor points out that the "formal perspective" of science fiction in general states that it fails to fulfill one of the criteria for realism, due to "the way in which sf deliberately deviates from the world-as-experienced in terms of its invented settings – that is, its use of non-mimetic contexts" ("Philip K. Dick and the Umbrella of Light", published by T-K Graphics, Baltimore, in 1975. Parts of it appeared earlier in the British journal *Foundation*, No. 4, July 1973, in an article entitled "Can God Fly? Can He Hold Out His Arms and Fly?" Reformatted and with minor corrections, 2019, p. 6). Taylor also discusses the sociological perspective, which looks at the implications of science fiction as a study of individuals who represent social groups and how they adapt to reality or fail to do so. Philip K. Dick's work definitely fits the sociological perspective, even as it fails to be mimetic in terms of consensus reality. However, his work does represent his personal reality, that is, reality as he saw it. Unlike the pillars of science fiction, such as H.G. Wells, Robert A. Heinlein, and Isaac Asimov, Philip K. Dick wove tales in which the external reality devolved into the internal fantasies and fears of individual characters; he used to describe that process at the evolution of a "silly putty universe".

Phil's experience of visions and his exploration of their meaning added fuel to the ongoing rumors that he was insane, that he had burned out his brains with drugs, that he was nothing but a raving madman who was no longer able to write. On the contrary, although he had not published any novels or stories in several years, he had been writing. He wrote half of his novel *Deus Irae* and sent the manuscript to his co-author Roger Zelazny in 1971. He wrote his novel *Flow My Tears, the Policeman Said* and gave the carbon copy of the manuscript to his divorce lawyer (an amazing example of foresight, or perhaps paranoia, which saved that novel from the ransacking of his home in 1971). He was in the process of writing a third novel, but the only copies of that manuscript were taken in the raid on his home on November 17, 1971. He never wrote that third novel. When he felt relatively safe in Fullerton in 1972, he began writing his next novel, *A Scanner Darkly*. He also submitted a number of letters and several short stories to various periodicals.

His science fiction novels and stories provide glimpses into his worldview, which hinges on the solid conviction that our world is not real. In fact, he maintained that our world is an informational matrix that hides reality behind a curtain of false images. In some sense, we are still living in the Roman Empire in the first century. Perhaps we are even the same people who lived in that time and place. We live in a false and limited reality, a simulation of objects, events and people. In his novels and stories, various characters perceive glimpses of the reality behind the simulation. Those characters lack a philosophical framework to organize their perceptions until the VALIS novels present Phil's model of reality.

He stated the core of his philosophical system in his 1977 speech in Metz, France:

> *We are living in a computer-programmed reality, and the only clue we have to it is when some variable is changed, and some alteration in our reality occurs. We would have the overwhelming impression that we were re-living the present – déjà vu – perhaps in precisely the same way: hearing the same words, saying the same words. I submit that these impressions are valid and significant, and I will even say this: such an impression is a clue, that in some past time-point, a variable was changed – re-programmed as it were – and that because of this, an alternative world branched off.*
> (quoted in Rizwan Virk, *The Simulation Hypothesis*. Bayview Books, 2019, p. 157. Also available for listening on numerous Youtube channels. Please note that this quotation is edited, and it is composed of snippets from different parts of the speech that Phil delivered.)

As Philip K. Dick wrote "in his journal in 1978 'we're in a *condition*, not a world'" (Philip K. Dick, *Exegesis*, p. 429; quoted in Amelia Barikin & Helen Hughes, Editors, *Making Worlds: Art and Science Fiction*. Victoria, Australia: Surpllus, 2013, p. 13).

As a result of that philosophical position, he was willing and able to believe two or more contradictory explanations of any phenomenon simultaneously. For example, the invasion of his house in November 1971 could have been a raid by federal authorities, a drug raid by local law enforcement, a burglary by drug addicts, a terrorist action by Black Panthers, Minute Men, the KKK, communists, a vindictive ex-wife, and so on and so forth, all at the same time. He contradicted himself on a regular basis, often stating that everything of value was taken from his home, yet at other times insisting that cash and other valuables were left behind, sitting out in plain sight. He claimed that his stereo equipment had been taken, but when a friend shipped his remaining possessions to our apartment in Fullerton, California, we found his stereo equipment among the boxes of books and record albums; however, his reel-to-reel tape recorder was not found among his possessions. Perhaps he had replaced the stereo equipment before going to Canada in early 1972, or perhaps it never was stolen at all. As the man himself used to ask, "Do you believe everything you're told?"

In any case, his house was invaded and torn apart, and his manuscripts and financial records were taken. A college student who visited shortly after the break-in took photographs and testified to the widespread damage. Windows were broken, doorknobs were knocked off of the doors, and an explosion had taken place in Phil's office. He always wondered, and never knew for certain, what he had done that led to this or who had carried it out.

That invasion of his home is the first X, the first major unknown, of his final decade of life. The Cross, which he believed to be in the form of the letter X, ran threadlike through his life from an early age, when his mother sent him to a boarding school run by Quakers. His friendship with Bishop James Pike led him to a more mature understanding of Christian faith, and even though Pike eventually concluded that the Resurrection was a lie, Phil continued to believe in Christ.

(NOTE: Bishop James Pike was tried for heresy by the Episcopal Church in 1969 for a radical interpretation of the virgin birth, and he agreed to step down from his position as Bishop of California. He is known for his book *The Other Side*, which documents his attempts to contact the spirit of his dead son, who committed suicide in 1966. He also detailed his church trial in a book titled *If This Be Heresy*. Pike died mysteriously in 1969, in the Israeli desert where he had traveled to find evidence that Jesus did not die on the Cross.)

~~~
~~~

CHAPTER THREE: NOVELS, STORIES AND FILMS

John Brunner called Philip K. Dick, ""The most consistently brilliant sf writer in the world" (John Brunner, "The Work of Philip K. Dick". *New Worlds* #166, vol. 50, 1966, p. 142). This was two years before the publication of *Do Androids Dream of Electric Sheep?* (1968, later known as Blade Runner), and possibly inspired by Phil's Hugo Award-winning novel *The Man in the High Castle* (1962) more than by his body of work at the time.

His mainstream novels were unpublished and unknown until they were released posthumously. Although those novels appear to be realistic, they often wander into absurdity, as well as the futility of life, reflecting the influences of Franz Kafka and Albert Camus. For example, we cannot be certain whether *In Milton Lumke Territory* tells the story of a grown man looking back on his childhood while he fails at selling typewriters, or the musings of an eleven-year-old boy imagining his future life as an adult. The open door to multiple interpretations of the same work characterizes his science fiction, as well.

His protagonists often fail at achieving their goals, but they usually find some consolation in a small victory. For example, at the end of *The Three Stigmata of Palmer Eldritch* (1965), Leo Bulero muses that we are not doing all that badly for an imperfect species which possesses little real power:

I mean, after all; you have to consider we're only made out of dust. That's admittedly not much to go on and we shouldn't forget that. But even considering, I mean it's a sort of bad beginning, we're not doing too bad. So I personally have faith that even in this lousy situation we're faced with we can make it. You get me?

Radio Free Albemuth (1985) ends in death for Nick Brady and what appears to be total defeat for Phil, until he comes to understand that young people represent a brighter future.

Radio Free Albemuth (1985, originally titled Valisystem A), which Phil wrote in 1974 but which was not published until three years after his death, verges on breaking out of science fiction into the mainstream of modern literature. The reader may feel free to conclude that Nick Brady is simply hallucinating, and that his diagnosis of his son's hernia stems from an unconscious recognition of the boy's symptoms and realization of what they mean. Even the secret society described by Sylvia could be taken as delusional, rather than actual. If that were the case, then everything else in the novel would be realistic, albeit dystopian, much after the pattern of an oppressive police state laid down by George Orwell in his novel *1984* or perhaps patterned after Ray Bradbury's *Fahrenheit 451*.

The Three Stigmata of Palmer Eldritch (1965) contributed to the rumors that Philip K. Dick was a heavy drug user. Another source of that misapprehension is Harlan Ellison's introduction to Phil's story "Faith of Our Fathers", which Ellison included in his anthology *Dangerous Visions* (1967), and in which Ellison falsely claimed that Phil wrote the story while under the influence of LSD. Phil's friend from high school and co-author of *The Ganymede Takeover* (1967), Ray Nelson, confirmed that Phil took LSD exactly two times. Nelson obtained the pharmaceutical drug from the research program at UCLA in the early 1960s. Phil wrote *Three Stigmata* before ever trying LSD, although he had read articles about that hallucinogenic pharmaceutical.

Three Stigmata presents Phil's fascination with dualism. Leo Bulero's product Can-D provides bored colonists on an alien world with an escape into a fantasy world for a short time. Palmer Eldritch's product Chew-Z spreads its creator into our world, taking over our reality and changing people into his own image.

Phil openly displayed the Zoroastrian scaffolding upon which he hung his cosmology in his early short story "A Glass of Darkness", which he expanded into his 1957 fantasy novel *The Cosmic Puppets*. The town of Millgate turns out to be the battle ground of the war between the forces of light and darkness. The protagonist gets trapped in the town, while his wife waits for him at a hotel bar in Washington, D.C. Christopher Sims points out that the typical hero in a Philip K. Dick story engages

in the cosmic fight against entropy" and that the world that the characters see is an illusion laid over the real world, hiding reality from our perception, and that the task of the hero is to uncover that underlying reality.
("The Ontological Task of the Hero in Philip K. Dick's *The Cosmic Puppets.*" 2018: *Journal of the Fantastic in the Arts*, 29.1, pp. 43-67).

Phil attempted to perform that same task of revealing the real world in his life, as well as in his art. He saw the Zoroastrian battle between light and darkness, good and evil, as a tangible reality. The Zoroastrian dualistic beliefs center around the battle between two deities: Ahura Maza the Lord of Light, and Ahriman the Lord of Darkness, so Phil strove to achieve enlightenment, to find the light that would reveal to him the real world behind the curtain of shadows. He believed that the Logos had transmitted information directly into his brain, showing him the reality of our imprisonment.

As Umberto Rossi and others have pointed out, Philip K. Dick explored the meaning and purpose of the Logos long before 1974. In Phil's 1959 novel *Time Out of Joint*, for example, the seemingly solid objects in Ragle Gumm's world turn out to be nothing more than words written on slips of paper. Rossi points out that Gumm begins to learn the truth of his situation from the words that he hears emanating from a child's crystal radio set.

(Note: The title "*Time Out of Joint*" is taken from Shakespeare's Hamlet, Act I, Scene 5, after the Ghost of

Hamlet's father tells his son that he was murdered. The Ghost vanishes, and Hamlet exclaims to his friend Horatio, "The time is out of joint.")

In response to critics who label Dick as a madman, Rossi states,

> There is much that Dick's earlier and later novels could say, and we should not shut them up by labeling them as the product of a madman. Even if they really were the product of a madman (as Artaud's and Van Gogh's works), they could still signify, speak to readers who are not crackpots or psychiatrists.
> (Umberto Rossi, "Just a Bunch of Words: The Image of the Secluded Family and the Problem of λογος in P. K. Dick's *Time Out of Joint*". *Extrapolation*, Vol. 37. No. 3, 1996: The Kent State University Press, p. 6).

Rossi insists that we must examine the text itself, not the author of the text. If that insistence summons a shadow of the philosophy of Postmodernism and "the death of the author" proposed by Roland Barthes, Rossi does not pursue it beyond the assertion that the author's mental state or psychiatric condition bears little or no relevance to the meaning of the text. In fact, he disputes the tenets of Postmodernism in his paper. Nevertheless, he holds that the novel itself tells us what we need to know: Objects revert to words written on slips of paper, and the illusion of reality fades away; the Logos, on the other hand, gives us a solid reality that does not revert to mere words.

(NOTE: see Roland Barthes, *Image-Music-Text*. London: Fontana, 1977, pp. 142-48)

When *Time out of Joint* (1959) depicts the protagonist, Ragle Gumm, discovering that many objects in his world are only words written on slips of paper, this foreshadows the appearance of words as salvific information in *UBIK*, a novel that Phil expanded from a short story titled "What the Dead Men Say". In some sense, *UBIK* presents the world of Plato's Cave, in which we see only the shadows of real objects and not those objects themselves. However, it also introduces the idea of salvation through information, when the Logos in the form of graffiti enters the world. Rather than dragging the characters out into the light, as Plato recommends, the Logos as Ubik uses information to coax people to find their own way out. That salvation through information does appear, on the surface, to be Gnostic. However, Phil conceived of salvation taking place in this world, for all of humanity and even all living things, whereas Gnosticism reserves their salvation for the few elite sages (all of them men, no women allowed) whose souls rise to the heavens and join the Pleuroma (the group of Aeons who emanated from the One).

Ubik, the mysterious life-saving substance in Philip K. Dick's novel *UBIK* (1969), represents divine intervention. Glen Runciter wields a spray can of Ubik while writing notes and graffiti to inform his dead employees that he will help them. Phil called Ubik a "sentient, perhaps a bioplasmic life form related to the Logos" (*Exegesis*, p. 67). He defines Ubik as "Salvific information penetrating through the 'walls' of our world by an entity with personality representing a life- and reality-supporting quasi-living force" (ibid. p. 275). This information might at first glance appear to be Gnostic in character, but that information fails to save Joe Chip and his companions from the entropy which takes their lives (or perhaps their afterlives).

At the beginning of the novel, Joe Chip and his colleagues believe that their boss, Glen Runciter, has been killed in an explosion. As their story progresses, however, Runciter informs them that he is alive and they are dead. Readers cannot be certain about Runciter's claim, but the objects in Joe Chip's world begin to degrade in strange ways. Rather than simply falling apart, they revert to previous forms. For example, when Joe Chip buys cigarettes, they are a brand that is not made any more. When he opens a pack of those cigarettes, they crumble into dust as if they were a hundred years old. When they try to find a phone number, they discover that the phone book is years out of date. Joe Chip buys a brand new tape recorder that he finds to be worn out from years of use. The year is 1992, but the brand new car that Joe buys is a 1939 LaSalle. We get only a few brief glimpses into Runciter's experience, where he is talking to his dead wife through a futuristic telephone attached to her cryogenic coffin. We are left to wonder whether Runciter is indeed alive, when he pulls a coin out of his pocket and finds that it displays a portrait of Joe Chip.

The Penultimate Truth (1964), expanded from the short story "The Defenders" (1953), offers a mundane reason why the world is not what it seems to be. The wealthy and powerful elite lead ordinary people to believe that they are fighting a global nuclear war, but they are actually providing luxuries for those who live in landed estates. Working people live underground, in the belief that high levels of radioactivity above ground would kill them. They produce "leadies" – lead robots – which turn out to be robot servants for the elite who live on the surface.

Now Wait for Last Year (1966) offers a more bizarre source for the illusory nature of this world. Aliens from a distant star have tricked us. Angus Taylor wrote in "The politics of space, time, and entropy" (Published in *Foundation 10*, June 1976, pp. 34–44)

> The real aliens of *Now Wait for Last Year* are also masters of illusion, masquerading as human. But their alienness lies not in their biology or their ecology but in their lack of empathy and compassion.
> (p. 39).

The novel also introduces a highly addictive drug, JJ-180, that causes people to travel in time. Apparently, Phil was obsessed with both drugs and time very early in his career. The lack of empathy among the aliens foreshadows his 1968 novel *Do Androids Dreams of Electric Sheep?*, in which androids are distinguished from humans by their lack of empathy.

When Ridley Scott made the film *Blade Runner* in 1982, he used a screenplay that was very loosely based on Phil's novel *Do Androids Dreams of Electric Sheep?* While that film was a box office flop, failing to make back the cost of production, it did bring the name of Philip K. Dick to the attention of Hollywood and the general public. Sadly, Phil did not live long enough to see the finished film or to enjoy his newfound fame and fortune.

Since then, a number of films have sprung from his novels and stories. *Total Recall*, based on the story "We Can Remember it for You, Wholesale", has been made twice. Both films stray far from the original story, but they were financially successful. *Minority Report*, based on a story of the same title, was a financial success, largely due to the box office appeal of the star, Tom Cruise. However, the film drastically changed the plot in which Phil had the psychics predicting that the protagonist would murder a top military officer. Instead, the film portrayed the predicted murder as a vengeance killing.

Screamers, based on the story "Second Variety", is an entertaining and underrated film in which the enemy creates bombs that look and act like humans. The seriously meaningful *Impostor* has also been largely ignored, even though it is both entertaining and thought-provoking.

On the very low budget end, *A Scanner Darkly* misses the point of Phil's novel, even though it remains technically faithful to the text of the novel. The film shows us that drugs are bad, but Phil's point was that the War on Drugs is evil.

Radio Free Albemuth is, in my opinion, the finest of all the films, in spite of its low budget. While deviating in places from the text of the novel, it achieves a high level of faithfulness to Phil's message. Rather than relying upon spectacular special effects, this film tells a story. We are living under a fascist regime, while believing that we are free citizens enjoying the peace and security provided by a benevolent government. We live in the Black Iron Prison, and the Empire never ended.

The first *Blade Runner* film (1982) did show that Rick Deckard's work was dehumanizing, even thought it presented more special effects than plot-advancing action. The second *Blade Runner* film (2019) has little to do with Phil's novel, other than the names of some of the characters. In the 1982 film, Rutger Hauer's monologue at the end captures the essence of what Phil was trying to achieve in his novel. Interestingly, Hauer wrote most of that speech himself. *Blade Runner 2049* (released in 2017) strays far from Phil's concept of empathy. Rather than questioning whether Rachel is a human who lacks empathy, the film questions whether Rick Deckard is a replicant.

CHAPTER FOUR: THE INVASION

Philip K. Dick's visionary experiences of 1974 came as a result of and relief from a pattern of harassment under which he had suffered for several years. Pushed to the extreme by authority figures and shadowy entities, and never knowing what he had done wrong, Phil found himself attempting suicide. He never knew who was after him or why, so he engaged in prolonged speculation involving neo-Nazis, the CIA, the FBI, President Nixon, the Black Panthers, the Minute Men and more. His novel *A Scanner Darkly*, which was inspired by his 1971 experiences in San Rafael, California, comes to the conclusion that the protagonist is spying on himself. The Marin County Sheriff actually accused him of having burglarized and trashed his own house, but it is highly unlikely that he did so. The devastation was quite obviously the work of several people, and it involved the use of explosives that Phil had no way of obtaining. As noted previously in this book, a college student from Fullerton visited that house and took photographs of the devastation, which was massive.

Phil thought that it might have had something to do with his friendship with Bishop James Pike, the renegade Episcopal Bishop of California who left the church in order to pursue evidence that Jesus did not die on the cross:

It seems most likely to me, after digesting information
which has recently come to my attention, that President
Nixon's Drug Enforcement Administration (DEA)
suspected him of criminal activity, including but not
limited to drug dealing. The invasion of his home on
November 17, 1971, appeared to be a search for drugs,
weapons and financial information. His bank statements
and tax returns were taken, along with the manuscripts
of his novels. All the food in his kitchen, including the
contents of his refrigerator, was tossed onto the floor.
Afterward, the Sheriff advised him to leave town, stating
that they didn't want his kind in Marin County, and
calling him a "crusader". Many young people hung out
at Phil's house in San Rafael, and many of them were
using illegal drugs, but that seemed insufficient to
trigger the huge response from authorities. The lingering
question was always, "Why and how did he come to the
attention of federal authorities, as opposed to or in
addition to local law enforcement?" I believe that I have
found the answer to that question.

The story of *The Exegesis of Philip K. Dick* begins on the first day of June in 1969, when John Lennon and Yoko Ono were holding their second "Bed-In for Peace" in a room at the Queen Elizabeth Hotel in Montreal, Canada. Accompanied by a number of visitors, they recorded the song "Give Peace a Chance" as part of their protest against the war in Vietnam. Among those visitors were a young journalist named Paul Williams, and an advocate for the psychiatric use of LSD named Dr. Timothy Leary (Susan Breslow Sardone, "The John Lennon/Yoko Ono Bed-In for Peace in Montreal." *tripsavvy,* Updated June 26, 2019. https://www.tripsavvy.com/john-lennon-yoko-ono-montreal-1860460).

Paul Williams decided to telephone his friend Philip K. Dick from that hotel room, and Leary also spoke to Paul's friend, telling him that he was a big fan of his science fiction stories. Paul Williams had given copies of Phil's novel *The Three Stigmata of Palmer Eldritch* to both Lennon and Leary. Paul Williams later confirmed to me that he had made that phone call. In conversations years later, Phil also claimed that John Lennon told him that the Beatles song "Paperback Writer" was about him. That phone call cheered up the impoverished writer of genre fiction whose marriage was falling apart. It also brought him to the attention of one or more agencies of the U.S. federal government.

The government most likely would not have had any interest in monitoring the telephone calls of an obscure author of pulp fiction, although Phil had signed a petition pledging to refuse to pay income taxes until the Vietnam War was ended. That petition was published in *Ramparts Magazine* in February 1968 (an image of that petition can be viewed at National War Tax Resistance Coordinating Committee https://nwtrcc.org/war-tax-resistance-resources/international-history-of-war-tax-resistance/1960s/). On the other hand, one or more government agencies most certainly would have monitored John Lennon's telephone calls. Even if they did not tap his telephone and listen to the calls, they would obtain records of the phone numbers for both incoming and outgoing calls. The hotel switchboard would keep those records in order to bill John Lennon for his use of their telephone lines, so they would be easily accessible to the authorities. This was long before the day of cellphones and internet, and there was no such thing as Voice Over Internet Protocol (VOIP). The fact that Dr. Leary was in the room on that day becomes important later in the timeline.

Phil's wife Nancy left him in the autumn of 1969, but her younger brother Michael continued living in the house. Phil was emotionally shattered by the loss of his wife and child, as well as physically broken by a recent attack of acute pancreatitis that had landed him in the hospital for over a week. He thought that he had taken some bad drugs. When the doctor refused to renew Phil's prescription for amphetamines, he said that he bought some meth tabs from Michael. However, later events have suggested that this was sheer coincidence. Phil suffered from gall stones and kidney stones, as well as other symptoms that were most likely related to chronic pancreatitis, a condition from which he suffered and all three of his children suffer. When he came home from the hospital, he decided not to use any drugs, including prescription drugs. The problem with that decision was that he suffered from chronic depression, a condition that had followed him from early childhood. Without medication, he became suicidal. Rather than take any direct action, he stopped taking medication for his high blood pressure, a condition which had kept him out of the draft for the Korean conflict. He was taking a big chance on suffering a stroke, and he could have died.

Phil's speculations often centered around a man calling himself Hal Kinchen (almost certainly not his real name). Kinchen had made sure that Phil was not at home when it was raided, and he tried to recruit Phil as some sort of courier for a shadowy organization that, he claimed, was so secret that not even the CIA knew about them. When Phil refused, Kinchen said that they (not he, himself, but others in his organization) would kill Phil and replace him with a look-alike. That organization would even write his novels and perhaps had already written a few. You will find this incident reflected in Phil's novel *Radio Free Albemuth* and the film of the same title. One thing is certain: Hal Kinchen phoned Phil and asked him to meet at a local coffee shop on November 17, 1971, insisting that it was very important that they should meet right away. After hanging up the phone, Phil realized that the coffee shop was a chain with two different locations near his home, and he didn't know which one Kinchen had meant when he asked for the meeting. He called back, but instead of saying hello, Kinchen answered the telephone by saying something that sounded like "Solarcon Six". After decades of trying to figure out what that might have meant, I conclude that it must have been a code word to let the others know that Phil was leaving the house, so they could search without interruption. Caller ID did not exist back then, so Kinchen might reasonably have thought that his cohorts were calling him.

Phil's car broke down on the freeway, so he never made it to the coffee shop. The next day, the mechanic told him that his car had been sabotaged. Phil and his girlfriend Stephanie had to wait for a tow truck and then take a taxi to get home. Oddly, the cab driver refused to take them to the house, saying that he was afraid to go into that neighborhood. He let them out on the corner a block away, and they had to walk the rest of the way. When they finally got back home, they found that the house had been torn apart. That home invasion was almost certainly related to Phil's contact with Dr. Timothy Leary.

On September 13, 1970, LSD advocate Dr. Timothy Leary escaped from California Men's Colony West, a minimum security prison where he had been serving an indeterminate sentence of six months to ten years on a conviction for drug charges. His prison clothes were later found in the restroom of a gas station about a mile away from the prison. This told the authorities that Leary had help, at least in the form of civilian clothing being provided for him ("Timothy Leary, Drug

Advocate, Walks Away From Coast Prison", September 14, 1970: *New York Times Archives*. https://www.nytimes.com/1970/09/14/archives/timothy-leary-drug-advocate-walks-away-from-coast-prison.html). In fact, Leary did have help, and he managed to leave the country and travel all over Europe as a sort of celebrity. President Nixon, who faced strong opposition to his policies, especially with regard to the war in Vietnam and the War on Drugs, had declared Leary "the most dangerous man in America" (Ari Shapiro, "Nixon's Manhunt For The High Priest Of LSD In 'The Most Dangerous Man In America'", *National Public Radio NPR*, January 5, 2018. https://www.npr.org/2018/01/05/575392333/nixons-manhunt-for-the-high-priest-of-lsd-in-the-most-dangerous-man-in-america and Michael S. Roth, "President Richard Nixon and LSD guru Timothy Leary, crazy in their own ways." *Washington Post*, January 12, 2018. https://www.washingtonpost.com/outlook/president-richard-nixon-and-lsd-guru-timothy-leary-crazy-in-their-own-ways/2018/01/12/76220fa4-ebf2-11e7-b698-91d4e35920a3_story.html)

The government certainly wanted the names and addresses of anyone who had any contact with Dr. Timothy Leary before he went to prison; they wanted to know who had helped him. There, on the lists of outgoing phone calls from John Lennon's hotel room, was the number of Philip K. Dick, who lived in Northern California (not too far from the prison where Dr. Leary had been held) and had signed a petition pledging to

withhold his income taxes as a protest against the war in
Vietnam. As Phil used to say, you don't have to be
important or even guilty of anything; all you have to do
is come to the attention of the authorities, and they will
hound you until they find a reason to arrest you. That is
what happened to him, aside from the fact that he never
was arrested. He fled to Canada, where he attempted
suicide and spent several weeks in a drug rehabilitation
facility called X-Kalay (a First Nations term meaning
"The Path"). Phil maintained that he had no memory of
swallowing the sleeping pills, but he must have done so,
since he woke up sitting on the floor next to an empty
water glass and an empty pill bottle. His complete
memory of that suicide attempt came back to him during
his March 1974 visions.

When he lay in bed in March 1974, hearing a
disembodied voice telling him to kill himself, he soon
realized that he had been forced to attempt suicide in
1972. The complete memory came back to him in a
dream-like vision. He had been invited to be the Guest
of Honor at a science fiction convention in Vancouver,
British Columbia, so that provided the poverty-stricken
author with an escape route from the harassment he
suffered in California. He decided to stay on in Canada
after the convention, and he rented an apartment. One
afternoon he was walking to a nearby pharmacy to get
some aspirin for a headache, and the next thing he knew,
he had swallowed 100 sleeping pills. They were
potassium bromide, recently dubbed the "date rape
drug", and at the time he said that you could purchase
them without a prescription, at least in Canada. But the

memory of what happened in between walking down the sidewalk and waking up in his apartment with an empty pill bottle had to be retrieved. The lost memory began coming back with a vision of his grandmother reaching into the kitchen cupboard for a blue-and-white box, while a soft male voice said, "It was the bromide."
When Phil told me about that vision, I thought that he had seen a box of Bromo Seltzer, a common remedy for heartburn that actually contained sodium bromide, a tranquilizer similar to potassium bromide, in its original formula. His grandmother "Meemaw" must have given him that medicine more than once during his childhood.

~~~
~~~

CHAPTER FIVE: THE VISIONS

In a letter (Paul Williams, Editor, *The Selected Letters of Philip K. Dick, 1977-1979*, Nevada City, CA: Underwood Books, 2010, p. 102) **Philip K. Dick wrote:**

> I have no doubt that it was the Holy Spirit, the Third Member of the Trinity, which took me over in a theolepsy in March of 1974, but in my notes and novel VALIS I am striving for new formulations, new and fresh ways of expressing what I believe to be the eternal truths, just as I did in MAZE OF DEATH and other earlier novels. As St. Augustine said, there is no end to the wonderful mystery of the Trinity; one can contemplate it for all eternity and yet not know it completely.
> (This passage can also be found at
> https://runkbaset.blogspot.com/2009/06/philip-k-dick-on-star-wars.html

Over a period of eight years, Philip K. Dick struggled to identify, define and explain what happened to him in 1974. Still reeling from the harassment he had suffered in 1971 and early 1972, he experienced the presence of a loving spirit that came down to console and protect him. The information content of his visions led him to identify that spirit as the Logos, that is, Christ as described in the first few verses of the Gospel of John:

1.	In the beginning was the Word, and the Word was with God, and the Word was God.

2.	The same was in the beginning with God.

3.	All things were made by him; and without him was not any thing made that was made.

4.	In him was life; and the life was the light of men.

5.	And the light shineth in darkness; and the darkness comprehended it not.

(King James Version)

Please note that "Word" is *Logos* in the original Greek, and it means much more than our English term "word". The Greek term for an ordinary word is *lexi*, as in our English word "lexicon". Logos is related to the English word "logic". In terms of the Gospel, Logos possesses or is the power of creation. Remember that in Genesis I, God said, "Let there be light", and he created the world that we know by speaking. Logos, in that context, is God's speech. In addition, the letter to the Hebrews, Chapter 11, verse 3, says, "Through faith we understand that the worlds were framed by the word of God, so that things which are seen were not made of things which do appear." This supports John's assertion that the Logos performed the Creation. In other words, the Logos is a person. For John, the word of God was Jesus Christ.

Carl Jung explained the Logos as the rational soul that guides the unconscious through a man's *anima*, while *Eros* (love) produces a woman's *animus*, stating, "The ancients called the saving word the Logos, an expression of divine reason. So much unreason was in man that he needed reason to be saved" (Carl Jung, *Liber Novus*, an unpublished manuscript that was translated by Mark Kyburz and published as a Red Book; New York: Norton, 2009, p. 280) and "On a low level the animus is an inferior Logos, a caricature of the differentiated masculine mind, just as on a low level the anima is a caricature of the feminine Eros. (Carl Jung, *Commentary Secret of the Golden Flower*, translated into English by Cary F. Baynes, a commentary on an ancient Chinese text that was first translated into German by Richard Wilhelm; New York: Harcourt Brace Jovanovich, 1929, 1970, p. 41). (Both of the above quotes can be found at Carl Jung Depth Psychology https://carljungdepthpsychologysite.blog/2019/06/05/carl-jung-on-logos-anthology/).

In other words, Logos produces Eros (Love) in the man's unconscious, while Eros produces Logos in the woman's unconscious. I find it odd and interesting that Jung chose the masculine god of love, Eros (Cupid), rather than the feminine goddess of love, Aphrodite (Venus), since the man's *anima* is supposed to be female.

Portrayals of the word of God as a person can be found in many places in the Old Testament. For example, in 1

Samuel, Chapter 3, verse 7, we find "Now Samuel did not yet know the Lord, neither was the word of the Lord yet revealed unto him." Since the books of the Old Testament were not written in Greek, "word" is not logos here (it is *dabar* or *davar*), but the "word of God" is presented as a person who is calling Samuel's name in Chapter 3:

1.   And the child Samuel ministered unto the Lord before Eli. And the word of the Lord was precious in those days; there was no open vision.

2.   And it came to pass at that time, when Eli was laid down in his place, and his eyes began to wax dim, that he could not see;

3.   And ere the lamp of God went out in the temple of the Lord, where the ark of God was, and Samuel was laid down to sleep;

4.   That the Lord called Samuel: and he answered, Here am I.

5.   And he ran unto Eli, and said, Here am I; for thou calledst me. And he said, I called not; lie down again. And he went and lay down.

6.   And the Lord called yet again, Samuel. And Samuel arose and went to Eli, and said, Here am I; for thou didst call me. And he answered, I called not, my son; lie down again.

7.   Now Samuel did not yet know the Lord, neither was the word of the Lord yet revealed unto him.

8.   And the Lord called Samuel again the third time. And he arose and went to Eli, and said, Here

am I; for thou didst call me. And Eli perceived
that the Lord had called the child.

9.   Therefore Eli said unto Samuel, Go, lie
down: and it shall be, if he call thee, that thou
shalt say, Speak, Lord; for thy servant heareth. So
Samuel went and lay down in his place.

10.   And the Lord came, and stood, and called
as at other times, Samuel, Samuel. Then Samuel
answered, Speak; for thy servant heareth.

11.   And the Lord said to Samuel, Behold, I will
do a thing in Israel, at which both the ears of
every one that heareth it shall tingle.

(King James version)

As the story tells us, the word of God is a person who
stands in the room with Samuel and speaks to him. In
verse 1 and verse 7, the text makes it clear that Samuel
sees the person standing before him – "there was no
open vision", but Samuel does see the Lord – and that
"the word of the Lord" was revealed to him in this
encounter or vision. Now, as a student of Eli, he must
have known the Scriptures, so the word of the Lord must
mean something else; it must mean the person who is
standing in the room and speaking to Samuel in verse
10. It could not be God himself, since even Moses was
not allowed to see God face to face because it would
surely kill him (see Exodus 33:18-20).

One might argue that the person standing in the room
with Samuel is the Angel of the Lord, but the text does
not say that. It says "the Lord". In other places in the
Old Testament, the text does name the Angel of the

Lord, and it can be argued that this Angel is God himself. However, the Angel of the Lord and the Lord sometimes appear together. One example is when Moses encounters the burning bush, and the Angel of the Lord speaks to him, and the Lord also speaks to him (Exodus 3:2-4). The Word, according to the Gospel of John, is Jesus Christ. Since Christ is God in human form, the Word is God in the form of a person.

The interpretation of the Word as a person is bolstered by seven of the prophets: Haggai, Jeremiah, Ezekiel, Hosea, Joel, Jonah, and Zephaniah:

Haggai 1:1-2

> 1.	In the second year of Darius the king, in the sixth month, in the first day of the month, came the word of the Lord by Haggai the prophet unto Zerubbabel the son of Shealtiel, governor of Judah, and to Joshua the son of Josedech, the high priest, saying,
> 2.	Thus speaketh the Lord of hosts, saying, This people say, The time is not come, the time that the Lord's house should be built.

Haggai clearly states that the word came to him and told him what God said. Thus, even though the word is not the same as God himself, it must be an aspect of the one God, or the belief that there is only one God falls apart and we have polytheism. Judaism is monotheist.

Six additional prophets at least imply that the word of God is a person:

Jeremiah 1:1-2
>1.	The words of Jeremiah the son of Hilkiah, of the priests that were in Anathoth in the land of Benjamin:
>2.	To whom the word of the Lord came in the days of Josiah the son of Amon king of Judah, in the thirteenth year of his reign.

Ezekiel 1:3
>The word of the Lord came expressly unto Ezekiel the priest, the son of Buzi, in the land of the Chaldeans by the river Chebar; and the hand of the Lord was there upon him.

Hosea 1:1
>The word of the Lord that came unto Hosea, the son of Beeri, in the days of Uzziah, Jotham, Ahaz, and Hezekiah, kings of Judah, and in the days of Jeroboam the son of Joash, king of Israel.

Joel 1:1
>The word of the Lord that came to Joel the son of Pethuel.

Jonah 1:1-2
>1.	Now the word of the Lord came unto Jonah the son of Amittai, saying,

2.   Arise, go to Nineveh, that great city, and cry against it; for their wickedness is come up before me.

       (NOTE: The word must be a person because he word is talking to him.)

Zephaniah 1:1

The word of the Lord which came unto Zephaniah the son of Cushi, the son of Gedaliah, the son of Amariah, the son of Hizkiah, in the days of Josiah the son of Amon, king of Judah.

As you can see, the word comes to these prophets and speaks to them. It is a person, and not merely the spoken or written words of God. The word is a member of the Godhead, the Trinity in Christian doctrine.

Gnosticism did not face the problem of the Word being God, or the doctrine of the Trinity, because it saw the various forms of deities as Archons and Emanations (Aeons), while the one God remained an impersonal force existing far away from the Earth and totally unconcerned with humanity. The Gnostics generallydo not equate Sophia (Wisdom) with the Logos (a separatee and higher emanation from the One), and she is not the Creator; she is not God. She gave birth to the Demiurge, an evil, inferior entity that created the material world (Stephan A. Hoeller (Tau Stephanus, Gnostic Bishop), "The Gnostic World View: A Brief Summary of Gnosticism," *The Gnosis Archive*, http://gnosis.org/gnintro.htm). This Demiurge ignorantly and pridefully proclaims himself to be the one and only God. While Gnosticism is dualistic in its concept of the material world versus the spiritual world, it does not refer to dualism in the sense of two supreme gods. In fact, the Gnostics believed in one God, and they believed that the one God did not care about us. (Edward Moore, "Gnosticism", *Internet Encyclopedia of Philosophy*. https://www.iep.utm.edu/gnostic/)

For Philip K. Dick, the Logos was not only the Word of God, but also his inspiration for writing. He had always sensed intuitively that our world is made of information and that our sensory perceptions filter that information to make it decipherable to our limited minds. The Logos, on the other hand, possesses and at the same time IS all information. For Gnostics, the Logos is the first and highest emanation from the One, and is separate from Sophia, from Jesus and from Christ.

In his *Exegesis*, Philip K. Dick presents the Logos as the outside source of living energy who corrects the disintegration of our world by supplying information (p. 5). He returns to this idea in a number of pages. In 1977, for example, he wrote about *UBIK*, "In the novel, information spontaneously intrudes into the world of the characters, indicating that their world is not what they think it is . . ." (*Exegesis*, p. 273). The editors of the *Exegesis* express concern about the apparent contradiction between information as both a force for order and a force for disorder, since information supplies entropy and thus should be considered a force for disorder, not order: "the quantity of 'surprise value' contained in any message [is defined] as its 'entropy'" (Editor's Note on p. 5; *The Exegesis of Philip K. Dick*).

That apparent contradiction stems from 20th-century mathematical communication theory, and it can be resolved through ancient philosophies, in particular among the Greeks. In fact, Phil himself turned to ancient Greek philosophers for much of his analysis of the Logos. Since Phil relied primarily on the *Encyclopedia Britannica*, I will make use of it here.

Looking at the works of Democritus and others, we find that perfect order (cosmos) is the same as perfect chaos, since we cannot observe anything when everything is the same. Perfect cosmos is a sea of sameness, and perfect chaos is also a sea of sameness. We might say that the quality of perfect cosmos is white light, while the quality of perfect chaos is black darkness, but both represent endless seas of nothing, or of everything but in which we can find nothing to observe. In other words, perfect cosmos requires a touch of chaos in order to produce the universe in which we live. That concept leads me to wonder what would happen if perfect chaos encountered a touch of cosmos. Would there be any difference?

In our world, cosmos and chaos exist in a delicate balance, and entropy is constantly but slowly upsetting that balance. Organisms die, rot and disappear, while new organisms are born to restore the balance, but they never quite achieve equilibrium. In the end, entropy will win because death and decay outweigh birth and growth, ever so slightly. Mountains rise and islands sink. Old stars die and new stars are born. Heat in one part of the universe is balanced by cold in another part of the universe, but one is always greater than the other, if only by a slight amount. Without this balance, in which one side slightly outweighs the other, the universe would soon devolve into either complete chaos or complete order (cosmos), and in the end we would not be able to distinguish between the two; that is, we would have no way of knowing whether we were observing complete chaos or complete cosmos.

In fact, we would not exist as we exist now, so we probably could not observe anything. Entropy is increasing as stars use up their energy and become cold relics of their former glory, and as newborn stars use up energy in order to light their fires. Entropy simply is not increasing fast enough to disrupt our daily lives. In the end, however, entropy will consume everything, leading to either complete cosmos or complete chaos. The universe will become a bubble of endless nothingness, with no stars, planets or galaxies, completely empty of any objects. However, all hope is not lost. Our universe might benefit from a source of energy that researchers are only beginning to postulate.

But first, what is our universe made of? Is it a collection of material objects suspended in a sea of nothingness? Is the vacuum of space really empty, or is it not a vacuum at all? Democritus posited that the void has as much existence as the material world. In other words, the vacuum of space possesses material existence, just as the matter which resides in the vacuum possesses material existence. This concept is reflected in the aether (or ether) model of space, proposed by Isaac Newton. It fell out of favor about 100 years ago when Einstein proposed his theories of relativity, but it is gaining new traction in the light of recent developments in astrophysics.

Newton needed to employ Plato's concept of a medium (aether) to explain the propagation of light, since he conceived of light as a wave similar to a sound wave, but 20th-century theories had light behaving as if each photon could be a particle that is capable of traveling through the vacuum. The concept of the aether is being resurrected as an alternative to dark matter. In current theories, the aether is modeled as a field, something like a magnetic field, rather than as a medium through which light travels in the way that sound waves travel through the air (See Zeeya Merali, "Ether returns to oust dark matter." *New Scientist*, August 23, 2006. Reprinted in EureekAlert. https://www.eurekalert.org/pub_releases/2006-08/ns-ert082306.php).

Democritus further asserted that all material is made of an infinite number of atoms (*atomon*), which are the smallest, indivisible bits of matter. Atoms, he said, come in different sizes, shapes and textures, but because they are all perfectly evenly distributed, all matter is essentially homogeneous until we perceive a difference in the sizes and textures of atoms that impinge on our senses. Since all the atoms are falling at a uniform rate in a uniform stream, we cannot perceive any difference or any thing. Only when a touch of chaos disrupts the uniformity do objects begin to appear in the universe.

Democritus formed his cosmology by elaborating and systematizing what he learned from his teacher Leucippus, who first proposed the theory of atomism, according to Aristotle and Theophrastus. (https://www.britannica.com/biography/Democritus ; https://www.britannica.com/biography/Leucippus)

Most of what we know about Democritus actually comes from fragments. We know more about the atomism of Epicurus through the Latin poet Lucretius, who developed the concept of *clinamen* in defense of Epicurus. In Books I and II of his magnum opus, *De Rerum Natura* (On the Nature of Things), Lucretius presents his atomic theory of the universe, and Book III presents his atomic theory of the soul. He posited that the universe is infinite, and that it is filled with an infinite number of atoms. Originally, the infinite number of atoms fell uniformly through infinite space, in perfect cosmos (order), until a single atom swerved and collided with another atom (https://www.britannica.com/biography/Lucretius). Lucretius gave the name *clinamen* to the tendency of the atoms to swerve (educalingo, Dictionary, "clinamen." https://educalingo.com/en/dic-en/clinamen). The uniform falling of atoms was everything and nothing at the same time. It was everything because the shower contained all the atoms in the universe. It was nothing because nothing could be observed, since everything was the same. Besides, there was no observer. Democritus did not believe in God, nor did he believe in any of the Greek gods, so he did not posit an entity outside the universe looking down on it and causing an atom to swerve. A tiny force or tendency caused a single atom to swerve ever so slightly, so it collided with another atom and began the touch of chaos that led to the creation of our universe, which we ironically call the cosmos. The original state of the atomic universe was total order (cosmos), and a touch of chaos led to everything that we observe.

If the force that we call entropy can be equated to the tendency to swerve which Lucretius called *clinamen*, then the apparent contradiction that disturbed the editors of *Exegesis* resolves itself. Basically, one atom slowed down slightly, and that tiny bit of entropy introduced the chaos that produced our cosmos. The very entropy which degrades our universe is the same force that created our universe. One might equate this to the introduction of entropy in the form of information by the Logos, a form of information that is both creative and destructive. Phil considered Ubik, the mysterious energetic substance in his novel *UBIK*, a form of the Logos. He wrote, "Precisely this world soul or logos appears in *UBIK* as the entity/force Ubik" (*Exegesis*, p. 394). He also equated the Logos with VALIS, a satellite in Earth orbit that transmits salvific information. In his *Exegesis*, Phil wrote, "My years of epistemological doubt, in which there was so much acosmism, was a search for true – or absolute or indubitable – being. I have found it in Ubik (i.e. Valis)" (p. 538), thus bringing together the two works under the umbrella of Logos.

In the universe that we perceive, entropy appears to degrade order into chaos, causing energy to drop down to increasingly less usable forms. Entropy, therefore, puts the brakes on the motion of all objects in the universe as they gradually lose access to the energy of motion. That energy continues to exist, but it changes into heat, a form of energy that is no longer kinetic and is therefore less useful, less efficient. In other words, the observed expansion of the universe from the Big Bang has been slowing down as entropy converts kinetic energy (the energy of motion) to heat, and eventually the universe loses heat and becomes cold. The heat does not actually cease to exist, but it becomes so evenly distributed that it cannot perform any work. In other words, the heat cannot heat up anything.

Our machines represent an attempt to reverse entropy, transforming heat energy into kinetic energy that we can use to move our automobiles, airplanes and other machinery. However, we never can achieve 100% efficiency with our conversion of heat to kinetic energy because we are working against the natural force of entropy. In the end, according to physicists, entropy will win. They call this the "heat death of the universe", and they base this concept on the second law of thermodynamics, which states that entropy will constantly increase in a closed system. Eventually, even heat will cease to exist in any meaningful sense because it will be perfectly evenly distributed throughout the universe, and therefore nonexistent because it cannot be observed any more than perfect cosmos could be observed.

For the religious, however, the universe is not a closed system. The Creator (or the Logos) reaches into our universe and adds energy in the form of information. For Philip K. Dick, Ubik (in his novel *UBIK*) represents that Logos (word) which recharges the batteries of our universe, so to speak, by adding information. Ironically, it was the same Word/Logos that created the Heavens and the Earth in the first chapter of Genesis, but which adds chaos to the cosmos. Thus, information both creates and destroys; it produces both cosmos and chaos, energy and entropy. For the religious, the Logos is the equivalent of the pagan concept of *clinamen*.

> Peter Fitting referred to the novel *UBIK* as a study of entropy ("*Ubik*: The Deconstruction of Bourgeois SF." *Science Fiction Studies*, March 1975. Available at (https://www.depauw.edu/sfs/backissues/5/fitting 5art.htm) Similarly, Phil wrote:

> In *UBIK* the forward-moving force of time (or time-force expressed as an ergic field) has ceased. All changes result from that. Forms regress. The substrate is revealed. Cooling (entropy) is allowed to set in unimpeded.
> (*Exegesis*, p. 3)

UBIK presents world in which dead people are cryogenically preserved in coffins that maintain their frozen state, and their loved ones can talk to them on futuristic telephones until they run out of energy and become completely dead. As the world of the dead degrades into cold chaos, a mysterious substance called Ubik reverses entropy by injecting energy into the system, thus increasing heat and order (cosmos). Ironically, heat is considered the lowest and least usable form of energy, that is, the form of energy containing the most entropy. For the characters who are freezing in Cold Pak, however, heat is a good thing. Their savior figure Glen Runciter adds Ubik to their world while also writing messages for them, thus adding information. It appears that something might be adding information or heat or both to our universe.

Recently, astrophysicists have observed an acceleration in the expansion of the universe. According to accepted theory, that expansion has been slowing down for about 5 billion years, since a short time after the Big Bang. Acceleration of the expansion should not happen if the universe is a closed system, but it is accelerating, as demonstrated by recent measurements of the Hubble constant, which is the rate of the expansion. It does not seem to be constant, after all. (Adam Mann, "No One Can Agree How Fast Universe is Expanding. New Measure Makes Things Worse", *Live Science*, https://www.livescience.com/hubble-constant-crisis-deepens.html). In other words, some sort of energy must be coming in from outside the universe, in order to cause the expansion to accelerate.

Attempting to explain this without resorting to theism, astrophysicists have brought in the concept of dark energy by resurrecting the cosmological constant which Einstein proposed in 1917 but later discarded based on the evidence from Edwin Hubble's observations of the expansion of the universe (Katie Mack, "Sorry, but the heat death of the universe is actually the nice option." April 9, 2019: *Cosmos, the Science of Everything.* https://cosmosmagazine.com/physics/sorry-but-the-heat-death-of-the-universe-is-actually-the-nice-option). We cannot detect dark energy, but it must be there, they say, because the expansion of the universe is accelerating.

(Similarly, astrophysicists have proposed that the universe is filled with "dark matter", which we cannot detect but which must be there because the galaxies should fall apart, based on the amount of detectable matter within them. However, if space is not a vacuum, but rather a medium – aether – or a field, then dark matter is not necessary to explain why galaxies do not fly apart.)

Phil did not know the term "dark energy", but he did perceive energy entering from outside our world, in the form of information. He called the source of this information the Logos. On page 4 of the *Exegesis*, he says, "Equilibrium is achieved by the Logos in three directions: from behind us as causal – time – pressure, from above, then the final form, the very weak H.S. drawing toward perfection each form" (Note: H.S. stands for Holy Spirit). In his novel *UBIK*, he called the source Ubik, a shortened from of "ubiquitous", a quality of God, who is everywhere at all times.

In his vision, he saw the Logos represented as "a gold and red illuminated-letter like [sic] plasmatic entity *from the future*, arranging bits and pieces here: arranging what time drove forward" (*Exegesis*, p. 5). He said that the red and gold illuminated letter looked like X, but it was something more than X, and he tried to draw it on a piece of paper. It was the Chi-Rho.

Phil equated this entity with the Logos, and also with Ubik, the life energy in a spray can from his novel *UBIK*, and with the alien satellite Valis from his novels *VALIS* and *Radio Free Albemuth,* which sends us information to set us free from the oppression and persecution of the Empire.

In terms of the "Big Bang" theory of the origin of the universe, a touch of chaos or *clinamen* is necessary to form the stars, planets and galaxies that we see today. If the cosmos had spread out evenly and in perfect symmetry from the point of its beginning, it would have formed a sphere of uniformly distributed energy or matter or both. It would resemble the uniform fall of atoms described in the theories of the ancient Greek philosophers. In other words, whatever spread out from the initial explosion that we call the "Big Bang", it did contain a bit of disorder. On the other hand, the "Big Bang" theory is supposedly proven by the detection of perfectly evenly distributed primordial energy at about 3 degrees above Absolute Zero, known as Cosmic Microwave Background (CMB) radiation.

Actually, a tiny bit of chaos has been found in the CMB. In recent years, researchers at NASA's Jet Propulsion Laboratory (JPL) have discovered that the CMB radiation is not perfectly distributed; they have found "fluctuations", and those fluctuations are not evenly distributed (California Institute of Technology, "What Came Before The Big Bang? Interpreting Asymmetry in Early Universe", Science News column, December 18, 2008: *Science Daily*. https://www.sciencedaily.com/releases/2008/12/081216131106.htm) This apparent contradiction between a slightly chaotic universe and the perfect cosmos of its origin needs more exploration.

Actually, the CMB did not come from the Big Bang itself, but resulted from a later development in the formation of our universe. Astronomers have been studying the oldest galaxies in our universe and concluded:

> In the early days of our cosmos, everything was pretty uniform: just about the same average density from place to place. . . .
> But all that chaos ended when the universe turned a ripe old 380,000 years old. [Matter spread out and cooled, enough to] form the first atoms of hydrogen and helium. With that event came the release of a tremendous amount of radiation that

we still know and love today: the cosmic microwave background.
(Paul Sutter, "When did the universe 'wake up'?" Space, Science and Astronomy, February 3, 2020, https://www.space.com/when-did-the-universe-wake-up.html)

This sounds a lot like the atomist theories of Democritus and Leucippus.

Phil experienced visions of the universe expanding under the guidance of God the Creator, that is the Logos.

~~~
~~~

CHAPTER SIX: THE CROSS IN THE SKY

The glowing red and gold letter (*Exegesis*, p. 5) that Phil saw hanging in midair in our dimly lit bedroom, and which he called the Logos, was the Chi-Rho. We did not know it at the time, but that is what Phil drew on a slip of paper back in 1974.

It first appeared in history in the year 312 when, on the eve of a crucial battle against the Western Roman emperor, Eastern Emperor Constantine ordered his troops to put a Christian symbol on their shields (J. M. Roberts, *History of the World*. New York: Oxford University Press, 1993, p. 227). Through common knowledge and various written histories, we are informed that Constantine saw a cross in the sky the night before the battle at Milvian Bridge on the River Tiber. Under the cross he read the words, "In hoc signo vinces", which means "conquer in this sign". He defeated his rival Maxentius in Rome, thus unifying the Eastern and Western Roman Empires. Phil learned about the battle by consulting his set of the *Encyclopedia Britannica* (https://www.britannica.com/topic/Battle-of-the-Milvian-Bridge).

The sign that Constantine saw was not the T-shaped cross which has become the most commonly accepted Christian symbol. Phil was halfway there when he declared that the cross was shaped like X, not T. The glowing letter that Phil saw in his vision was not a simple X, and he did not recognize it. The Chi-Rho was not generally known to lay people, although it was familiar to Biblical scholars and some historians. This is the symbol that Phil saw in his vision, and which Emperor Constantine saw the night before his crucial battle:

Chi-Rho. In hoc signo vinces.

Phil never found this information about the "cross" that Constantine say in the sky. He would have found his red-and-gold glowing letter, if he had pursued it. Instead, he speculated that the Cross was in the shape of the letter X, although he could find no support for his idea.

"Emperor Constantine won the Battle of Milvian Bridge and believed he won because of the symbol of Christ, the Chi Rho, upon the shields of his men" ("The Chi Rho Symbol", *Early Church History*. (https://earlychurchhistory.org/christian-symbols/the-chi-rho-symbol/). This is believed to be the first use of the Chi-Rho, which represents the first two letters of the word Christ in the Greek alphabet. Another possibility is that the Chi-Rho stands for Christ Reigns, *Christos Rhegas.*

Constantine and succeeding emperors issued coins with the Chi-Rho symbol embossed on them. On some of those coins, the Chi-Rho is flanked by the Greek letters Alpha and Omega, the first and last letters of the Greek alphabet ("Christian Symbols on Roman Coins", *Augustus Coins*. http://augustuscoins.com/ed/Christian/ChristianSymbols. html), which we associate with the statement in the New Testament that Christ is "the Alpha and the Omega, the first and the last, the beginning and the end" (Revelation 22:13).

Constantine displayed the "labarum" in subsequent battles. Phil could have found more information in his encyclopedia, if he had searched for the meaning of the labarum:

> **Labarum**, sacred military standard of the Roman emperors, first used by Constantine I in the early part of the 4th century AD. The labarum—a Christian version of the vexillum, the military standard used earlier in the Roman Empire—incorporated the Chi-Rho, the monogram of Christ, in a golden wreath atop the staff. The flag was made of purple silk (purple dye being at this time a rarity derived from a shellfish of the genus *Murex*) richly embroidered with gold.
>
> *("Labarum", Encyclopedia Britannica.* https://www.

)
Shape of the cross: T or X?

Phil speculated that the cross on which Jesus died was shaped like X, rather than T, but this is highly unlikely. The consensus among experts is that it was shaped like the letter T. There are four known types of crosses used for crucifixion. The "Crux Simplex" was a simple stake with no cross pieces, but Jesus probably was not hanged on that type of cross because more than one nail was used to hold his hands. J. Warner Wallace writes that, since Thomas asked to see "the holes from the nails" that pierced Jesus's hands, the "Crux Simplex" is not a likely candidate, since "he would likely have had his hands nailed in place with a single stake" ("What Was the Shape of Jesus' Cross?" *Cold Case Christianity*. https://coldcasechristianity.com/writings/what-was-the-shape-of-jesus-cross/). "Doubting" Thomas referred to more than one nail, not a single stake.

The "Crux Commissa" or "Tau Cross" is shaped like the upper case letter T, with the horizontal cross-piece on top of the post. The "Crux Immissa," is shaped like the lower case letter t, with the post extending for a short distance above the horizontal cross-piece. The "Crux Decussata" is shaped like the letter X. Wallace turns to the Gospels of Matthew and Luke for clarification as to the most likely shape of the cross, focusing on the sign that was placed above Jesus's head as he hung from the cross:

Matthew 27:37

And over His head they put up the charge against Him which read, "This is Jesus, the King of the Jews."

Luke 23:38

Now there was also an inscription over Him, "This is the King of the Jews."

Wallace then refers to John 19:20, which says: "Many of the Jews read this inscription, for the place where Jesus was crucified was near the city, and it was written in Aramaic, in Latin, and in Greek" (Note: Wallace paraphrases the verse, but I quote it here in full. Wallace used the New International Version (NIV), but here I have used the English Standard Version (ESV). The differences are trivial, being "above" instead of "over", and the use of all upper case letters for the words of the sign in the NIV).

The "Crux Decussata", shaped like the letter X, could not accommodate the sign above Jesus' head, so the Cross must have been shaped like the letter T. Wallace concludes that the "Crux Commissa" is the best candidate for the Cross, since it is in his opinion the only shape that fits the placement of the sign over Jesus's head. The "Crux Commissa" is the shape of the upper case letter T, with the cross-piece on top of the post. I submit that the "Crux Immissa," which is shaped like lower case t, would serve as well or better, with the sign attached to the top of the post, rather than the words inscribed on the cross piece where Jesus' arms were nailed to the cross. His head would be in the way of the sign on the cross if it was shaped like the upper case T. In any case, the "Crux Decussata", which is shaped like the letter X, would not do for the placement of the sign above Jesus's head.

~~~
~~~

CHAPTER SEVEN: DUALISM IN THE EXEGESIS

CHAPTER EIGHT: WE ARE THE EARLY CHRISTIANS

Phil drew some of his theology from C.S. Lewis' book *Mere Christianity*, but where Lewis used metaphor, Phil took those statements as literal truth. In the final chapter, Lewis says that we are the early Christians, but where he meant that two thousand years are just a blink of the eye in the history of life on Earth, Phil took it to mean that we are actually the same people and that we are living in the first century of the Christian era.

~~~

Notes for further study.

~~~

mimesis

koinos kosmos

idios kosmos

"Freud's theorizings on the unconscious and Einstein's

theories of relativity questioned the possibility of there being a fixed version of reality which could be described as objective."
(Butler Chapter 1, p. 10)
("Ontology and Ethics in the Writings of Philip K Dick") Univeristy of Hull, 1995

~~~

Bohemian Grove (*Exegesis*, p. 15) & owl (p. 16)

phantasmagoria – shifting images

Entelechy
information virus William S. Burroughs latent meaning-extraction method
Bateson's immanent mind
incised form
labarum = chi plus rho; Constantine used it

hypostasis

google says "The labarum was a vexillum that displayed the "Chi-Rho" symbol ☧, a christogram formed from the first two Greek letters of the word "Christ" — Chi and Rho. It was first used by the Roman emperor Constantine the Great. Wikipedia"

and "The vexillum was a flag-like object used as a military standard by units in the Ancient Roman army. Wikipedia "
~~~

"a subdivision of a Roman legion, containing either 120 or 60 men.
1.2.
  (in church use) a vestment formerly worn by a priest celebrating the Eucharist, consisting of a strip hanging from the left arm."

porcupine tree – music group band

 the hooked X – Kensington rune stone and Henry Sinclair and Knights Templar and Columbus's signature and X is Roman numeral 10
ontogeny recapitulated phylogeny

dark the absence of light

time moves forward because the universe is expanding; time will reverse when the universe contracts

Ontology and Phylogeny

Biologists once believed that the developing embryo repeats the progress of the evolution of species from a single-celled organism to various multi-cellular organisms: to fish, amphibians, reptiles, mammals, and finally the apex of the evolutionary process, man. This theory was expressed in the statement, "Ontogeny is the abbreviated recapitulation of phylogeny." Of course, this theory has been thoroughly debunked, but it still can serve as a useful metaphor.

In VALIS, for example, Horselover Fat begins as an infant in terms of religion, and he progresses through various stages of enlightenment.

Twin Deities, Twin Universes

God contained all pairs of opposites, so in a sense God did not exist because the opposites canceled each other, leaving nothing that could be observed. In fact, no observer existed to attempt to see God. In the sense that God could not be observed, God was no thing, or nothing, and did not exist, at least not in a way that we could understand. In order to fulfill the desire to exist, God divided itself into two parts, one containing the active aspects of Deity, the other containing the passive aspects of Deity. Like the yin-yang symbol of Taoism, each part contained a small amount of the other part. In other words, the active half contained a small portion of the passive, and the passive half contained a small part of the active. This was done so each half of God would remember the other half, since each had a small portion of the other as a reminder.

Since each twin contains the opposite of the other twin, and since God is everything, one twin contains existence, while the other contains nonexistence. In other words, the active twin exists and contains a small amount of nonexistence, while the passive twin does not exist and contains a small amount of existence.

Our universe exists in a narrow swath where the twin universes formed by the splitting of the Deity overlap. They are not completely separate, and each is aware of the other. Each half of the Deity is also aware of our existence.

Apollo/Apollyon the Shining One

Apollo is not the sun god, although he has been confused with such a deity. The sun god is Helios, who drives the chariot of the Sun across the sky. Apollo is Phoebus, the Shining One, the enemy called Apollyon in John's Revelation. Like the shining angel described by Isaiah, Apollo is cast down to the Earth.

Empedocles, ancient secrets/mysteries
Asklepios raised the dead, was killed by a cyclops.

Metanoia

https://www.space.com/what-is-the-black-knight.html

VALIS = Black Knight?
The fact that we don't have a confirmed explanation of their cause, however, has been seized upon: In 1973, Duncan Lunan wrote an article in Spaceflight magazine suggesting those studying long delayed echoes had overlooked the possibility they were sent by an alien space probe.

Lunan still has faith in an extraterrestrial explanation for the recordings. "The changes in the long distance echo patterns in apparent response to changes in the outgoing signals from Earth really do look like the responses of a Bracewell probe, and there is still no satisfactory natural explanation for the phenomenon," Lunan said. If the long distance echoes were deliberately produced by a probe, there's a problem in that they stopped in 1975.

"If a probe was monitoring Earth, rather than trying to attract attention, perhaps it belatedly discovered from the 1973 to 1974 publicity that it had given away its presence in the 1920s and pulled out in 1975," Lunan said. "That's the only explanation I can see for its apparent departure."

And yet, for all of that, Lunan said his research has nothing to do with the "Black Knight nonsense." If there is a link between his theory and the Black Knight, it is not one that is being made by him.

Elijah brought a boy back to life and then disappeared in a whirlwind.

Schopenhauer, this cat is the same as the cat 200 years ago. Cf: Plato's forms.

~~~

Translations of the Nag Hammadi Library (Gnostic texts found in Egypt in 1945) were not widely available until 1978, when James Robinson's book *The Nag Hammadi Library* was published in 1978. That having been said, Philip K. Dick had some passing knowledge of their content through his friendship with Bishop Pike.

~~~